The Perfect Christmas Carol Lyric Book

Traditional Carols Compiled by

James Isaac

Hello Fellow Singer,

Happy Holidays and Merry Christmas!

One of our favorite holiday tradition is caroling with our friends and family. We compiled this book to make it easier to sing with a group.

We hope this collection of fun and festive Christmas Carols will bring joy to you and your kin this holiday season. All these songs are in the public domain, so they can be sung freely. The songs in this book have been organized alphabetically.

Have a lovely holiday season and happy singing!

James Isaac

Table of Contents

Angels We Have Heard on High

(Verse)

Angels we have heard on high
Sweetly singing o'er the plains,
And the mountains in reply
Echoing their joyous strains.

(Chorus)

Gloria in excelsis Deo.

Gloria in excelsis Deo.

(Verse)

Shepherds, why this jubilee?
Why your joyous strains prolong?
What the gladsome tidings be
Which inspire your heav'nly song?

(Chorus)

Gloria in excelsis Deo.

Gloria in excelsis Deo.

(Verse)

Come to Bethlehem and see
Him whose birth the angels sing;
Come, adore on bended knee
Christ the Lord, the newborn King.

(Chorus)

Gloria in excelsis Deo.

Gloria in excelsis Deo.

Text: French carol, ca. 1862
Music: French carol

Auld Lang Syne

(Verse)

Should auld acquaintance be forgot,
And never brought to mind?
Should auld acquaintance be forgot,
And auld lang syne?

(Chorus)

For auld lang syne, my dear,
For auld lang syne,
We'll take a cup of kindness yet,
For auld lang syne.

(Verse)

And surely you'll buy your pint cup!
And surely I'll buy mine!
And we'll take a cup o' kindness yet,
For auld lang syne.

(Chorus)

We two have run about the slopes,
And picked the daisies fine;
But we've wandered many a weary foot,
Since auld lang syne.

(Verse)

We two have paddled in the stream,
From morning sun till dine;
But seas between us broad have roared
Since auld lang syne.

(Chorus)

And there's a hand my trusty friend!
And give me a hand o' thine!
And we'll take a right good-will draught,
For auld lang syne.

Text: Robert Burns, ca. 1788.
Music: Scottish Traditional Tune, ca. 1799.

Away In the Manger

Away in a manger, no crib for his bed,
The little Lord Jesus laid down his sweet head.
The stars in the bright sky looked
down where he lay,
The little Lord Jesus asleep on the hay.

The cattle are lowing; the baby awakes,
But little Lord Jesus, no crying he makes.
I love thee, Lord Jesus; look down from the sky
And stay by my cradle till morning is nigh.

Be near me, Lord Jesus; I ask thee to stay,
Close by me forever, and love me, I pray.
Bless all the dear children in thy tender care,
And fit us for heaven to live with thee there.

Text: Anon., ca. 1882, Philadelphia.
Music: "Cradle Song" by William J. Kirkpatrick.

Bring a Torch, Jeanette Isabella

(Verse)

Bring a torch, Jeanette, Isabella
Bring a torch, to the cradle run!
It is Jesus, good folk of the village;
Christ is born and Mary's calling;
Ah! ah! beautiful is the Mother
Ah! ah! beautiful is her Son!

(Verse)

It is wrong when the Child is sleeping
It is wrong to talk so loud;
Silence, all, as you gather around.
Lest your noise should waken Jesus.
Hush! hush! See how fast He slumbers!
Hush! hush! See how fast He sleeps!

(Verse)

Hasten now, good folk of the village;
Hasten now the Christ Child to see.
You will find Him asleep in the manger;
Quietly come and whisper softly,
Hush! hush! Peacefully now He slumbers.
Hush! hush! Peacefully now He sleeps.

(Verse)

Softly to the little stable.
Softly for a moment come;
Look and see how charming is Jesus
How He is white, His cheeks are rosy!
Hush! hush! see how the Child is sleeping;
Hush! hush! see how He smiles in his dreams.

Text: Emile Blemont, Translated by Edward Cuthbert Nunn,
CA. 1900.
Music: French traditional carol.

Coventry Carol

Lullay, thou little tiny child,
Sleep well, lully, lullay.
And smile in dreaming, little one,
Sleep well, lully, lullay.

Oh sisters two, what may we do,
To preserve on this day.
This poor youngling for whom we sing,
Sleep well, lully, lullay,
Farewell, lully, lullay.

Herod the king in his raging,
Set forth upon this day.
By his decree, no life spare thee,
All children young to slay,
All children young to slay.

Then woe is me, poor child, for thee,
And ever mourn and say.
For thy parting, neither say nor sing,
Farewell, lully, lullay,
Farewell, lully, lullay.

And when the stars fill darkened skies,
In their far venture, stay.
And smile as dreaming, little one,
Farewell, lully, lullay,
Dream now, lully, lullay.

Text: Robert Croo, ca. 1534.

Music: Traditional Tune, ca. 1591.

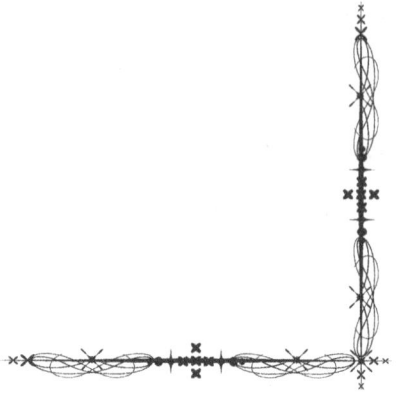

Deck the Halls

Deck the halls with boughs of holly,
Fa-la-la-la-la, la-la-la-la.
'Tis the season to be jolly,
Fa-la-la-la-la, la-la-la-la.
Don we now our gay apparel,
Fa-la-la, la-la-la, la-la-la.
Troll the ancient Yule-tide carol,
Fa-la-la-la-la, la-la-la-la.

See the blazing Yule before us,
Fa-la-la-la-la, la-la-la-la.
Strike the harp and join the chorus,
Fa-la-la-la-la, la-la-la-la.
Follow me in merry measure,
Fa-la-la, la-la-la, la-la-la.
While I tell of Yule-tide treasure,
Fa-la-la-la-la, la-la-la-la.

(Verse)

Fast away the old year passes,
Fa-la-la-la-la, la-la-la-la.
Hail the new year, lads and lasses,
Fa-la-la-la-la, la-la-la-la.
Sing we joyous, all together,
Fa-la-la, la-la-la, la-la-la.
Heedless of the wind and weather,
Fa-la-la-la-la, la-la-la-la.

Text: Thomas Oliphant, ca. 1862.

Music: Welsh Traditional. ca. 16th century.

The First Noel

(Verse)

The First Noel the angel did say
Was to certain poor shepherds
In fields as they lay;
In fields as they lay, keeping their sheep,
On a cold winter's night that was so deep.

(Chorus)

Noel, Noel, Noel, Noel,
Born is the King of Israel.

(Verse)

They looked up and saw a star
Shining in the east beyond them far,
And to the earth it gave great light,
And so it continued both day and night.

(Chorus)
Noel, Noel, Noel, Noel,
Born is the King of Israel.

(Verse)
And by the light of that same star
Three wise men came from country far;
To seek for a king was their intent,
And to follow the star wherever it went.

(Chorus)
Noel, Noel, Noel, Noel,
Born is the King of Israel.

(Verse)
This star drew nigh to the northwest,
O'er Bethlehem it took it rest,
And there it did both stop and stay
Right over the place where Jesus lay.

(Chorus)
Noel, Noel, Noel, Noel,
Born is the King of Israel.

(Verse)

Then entered in those wise men three
Full reverently upon their knee,
and offered there in his presence
Their gold, and myrrh, and frankincense.

(Chorus)

Noel, Noel, Noel, Noel,
Born is the King of Israel.

(Verse)

Then let us all with one accord
Sing praises to our heavenly Lord;
That hath made heaven and earth of naught,
And with his blood mankind hath bought.

(Chorus)

Noel, Noel, Noel, Noel,
Born is the King of Israel.

Text: Cornish. Edited by William Sandys, ca. 1823.
Music: Traditional English Carol.

Go Tell It on the Mountain

(Chorus)

Go, tell it on the mountain,
Over the hills and everywhere.
Go, tell it on the mountain,
That Jesus Christ is born.

(Verse)

While shepherds kept their watching,
O'er silent flocks by night.
Behold throughout the heavens,
There shone a holy light.

(Chorus)

Go, tell it on the mountain,
Over the hills and everywhere.
Go, tell it on the mountain,
That Jesus Christ is born.

(Verse)

The shepherds feared and trembled,
When lo above the Earth.
Rang out the angel's chorus,
That hailed our Savior's birth.

(Chorus)

Go, tell it on the mountain,
Over the hills and everywhere.
Go, tell it on the mountain,
That Jesus Christ is born.

(Verse)

Down in a lowly manger,
Our humble Christ was born.
And God sent us salvation,
That blessed Christmas morn.

(Chorus)

Go, tell it on the mountain,
Over the hills and everywhere.
Go, tell it on the mountain,
That Jesus Christ is born.

Text: John Wesley Work Jr., ca. 1865.

God Rest Ye Merry Gentlemen

(Verse)

God rest ye merry gentlemen,
Let nothing you dismay,
Remember Christ our Savior
Was born on Christmas Day;
To save us all from Satan's power
When we were gone astray.

(Chorus)

O tidings of comfort and joy,
Comfort and joy,
O tidings of comfort and joy!

(Verse)

From God our heavenly Father
A blessed angel came;
And unto certain shepherds
Brought tiding of the same;
How that in Bethlehem was born
The Son of God by name.

(Chorus)

O tidings of comfort and joy,
Comfort and joy,
O tidings of comfort and joy!

(Verse)

"Fear not, then," said the angel,
"Let nothing you affright;
This day is born a Savior
Of a pure virgin bright,
To free all those who trust in him
From Satan's power and might."

(Chorus)

O tidings of comfort and joy,
Comfort and joy,
O tidings of comfort and joy!

(Verse)

Now to the Lord sing praises,
All you within this place,
And with true love and brotherhood
Each other now embrace;
this holy tide of Christmas
Doth bring redeeming grace.

(Chorus)

O tidings of comfort and joy,
Comfort and joy,
O tidings of comfort and joy!

Text: English Traditional Carol, ca. 1760.
Music: Unknown.

Good King Wenceslas

Good King Wenceslas looked out,
On the Feast of Stephen.
When the snow lay round about,
Deep and crisp and even.
Brightly shone the moon that night,
Though the frost was cruel.
When a poor man came in sight,
Gathering winter fuel.

Hither, page, and stand by me,
If thou knowst it, telling.
Yonder peasant, who is he?
Where and what his dwelling?
Sire, he lives a good league hence,
Underneath the mountain.
Right against the forest fence,
By Saint Agnes fountain.

Bring me flesh and bring me wine,
Bring me pine logs hither.
Thou and I shall see him dine,
When we bear them thither.
Page and monarch, forth they went,
Forth they went together.
Through the rude winds wild lament,
And the bitter weather.

Sire, the night is darker now,
And the wind blows stronger.
Fails my heart, I know not how,
I can go no longer.
Mark my footsteps, good my page,
Tread thou in them boldly.
Thou shall find the winters rage,
Freeze thy blood less coldly.

In his masters step he trod,
Where the snow lay dinted.
Heat was in the very sod,
Which the Saint had printed.
Therefore, Christian men, be sure,
Wealth or rank possessing.
Ye, who now will bless the poor,
Shall yourselves find blessing.

Text: John Mason Neale, ca. 1853.

Hark, the Herald Angels Sing

(Verse)

Hark the herald angels sing,
Glory to the newborn King.
Peace on earth and mercy mild,
God and sinners reconciled.

(Chorus)

Hark the herald angels sing,
Glory to the newborn king.

(Verse)

Joyful all ye nations rise,
Join the triumph of the skies.
With angelic host proclaim,
Christ is born in Bethlehem.

(Chorus)

Hark the herald angels sing,

Glory to the newborn king.

(Verse)

Hail the Heaven born Prince of peace,
Hail the Son of righteousness.
Light and life to all He brings,
Risen with healing in His wings.

(Chorus)

Hark the herald angels sing,
Glory to the newborn king.

Mild He lays His glory by
Born that Man no more may die
Born to raise the sons of earth
Born to give them second birth

(Chorus)

Hark the herald angels sing,
Glory to the newborn king.

Text: Charles Wesley, ca. 1770.

Music: Felix Mendelssohn, ca. 1830.

Here We Come A-Caroling

(Verse)

Here we come a-caroling,
Among the leaves so green!
Here we coma a-wandering,
So fair to be seen!

(Chorus)

Love and joy come to you,
And to you glad Christmas too,
And God bless you and send you,
A Happy New Year,
And God send you a Happy New Year!

(Verse)

We are not daily beggars,
That go from door to door!
But we are friendly neighbours,
Whom you have seen before!

(Chorus)

Love and joy come to you,
And to you glad Christmas too,
And God bless you and send you,
A Happy New Year,
And God send you a Happy New Year!

(Verse)

We have got a little purse
Of stretching leather skin.
We want a little of your money,
To Line it well within.

(Chorus)

Love and joy come to you,
And to you glad Christmas too,
And God bless you and send you,
A Happy New Year,
And God send you a Happy New Year!

(Verse)

God bless the master of this house,
Likewise the mistress too.
And all the little children,
That round the table go.

(Chorus)

Love and joy come to you,
And to you glad Christmas too,
And God bless you and send you,
A Happy New Year,
And God send you a Happy New Year!

Text: Unknown, ca. 19th century.

The Holly and the Ivy

(Verse)

The holly and the ivy,
When they are both full grown,
Of all the trees that are in the wood,
The holly bears the crown.

(Chorus)

The rising of the sun,
And the running of the deer,
The playing of the merry organ,
Sweet singing in the choir.

(Verse)

The holly bears a blossom,
As white as lily flow'r,
And Mary bore sweet Jesus Christ,
To be our sweet Saviour.

(Chorus)

The rising of the sun,
And the running of the deer,
The playing of the merry organ,
Sweet singing in the choir.

(Verse)

The holly bears a berry,
As red as any blood,
And Mary bore sweet Jesus Christ,
To do poor sinners good.

(Chorus)

The rising of the sun,
And the running of the deer,
The playing of the merry organ,
Sweet singing in the choir.

(Verse)

The holly bears a prickle,
As sharp as any thorn,
And Mary bore sweet Jesus Christ,
On Christmas Day in the morn.

(Chorus)

The rising of the sun,
And the running of the deer,
The playing of the merry organ,
Sweet singing in the choir.

(Verse)

The holly bears a bark,
As bitter as any gall,
And Mary bore sweet Jesus Christ,
For to redeem us all.

(Chorus)

The rising of the sun,
And the running of the deer,
The playing of the merry organ,
Sweet singing in the choir.

(Verse)

The holly and the ivy,
When they are both full grown,
Of all the trees that are in the wood,
The holly bears the crown.

Text: Traditional English. Ca. 19th Century.

I Heard the Bells on Christmas Day

I heard the bells on Christmas day
Their old familiar carols play;
In music sweet the tones repeat,
"There's peace on earth, good will to men."

I thought how, as the day had come,
The belfries of all Christendom
Had rolled along th' unbroken song
Of peace on earth, good will to men.

And in despair I bowed my head:
"There is no peace on earth," I said,
"For hate is strong, and mocks the song
Of peace on earth, good will to men."

Then pealed the bells more loud and deep:
"God is not dead, nor does He sleep,
For Christ is here; His Spirit near
Brings peace on earth, good will to men."

When men repent and turn from sin
The Prince of Peace then enters in,
And grace imparts within their hearts
His peace on earth, good will to men.

O souls amid earth's busy strife,
The Word of God is light and life;
Oh, hear His voice, make Him your choice,
Hail peace on earth, good will to men.

Then happy, singing on your way,
Your world will change from night to day;
Your heart will feel the message real,
Of peace on earth, good will to men.

Text: Henry Wadsworth Longfellow, ca. 1864.

Music: John Baptiste Calkin, ca. 1872.

I Saw Three Ships

(Verse)

I saw three ships come sailing in,
On Christmas day, on Christmas day.
I saw three ships come sailing in,
On Christmas day in the morning.

(Verse)

And who do you think was in them then?
On Christmas day, on Christmas day.
And who do you think was in them then?
But Joseph and his lady.

(Verse)

He did whistle and she did sing,
On Christmas day, on Christmas day.
He did whistle and she did sing,
On Christmas day in the morning.

(Verse)

And all the bells on earth did ring,
On Christmas day, on Christmas day.
And all the bells on earth did ring,
On Christmas day in the morning.

(Verse)

And all the angels in heaven did sing,
On Christmas day, on Christmas day.
And all the angels in heaven did sing,
On Christmas day in the morning.

(Verse)

I saw three ships come sailing in,
On Christmas day, on Christmas day.
I saw three ships come sailing in,
On Christmas day in the morning.

Text: - Traditional English Carol, ca. 17th century. Published in 1833 by William Sandys.

Music: - Traditional tune of "As I sat on a sunny bank."

In the Bleak Midwinter

In the bleak mid-winter
Frosty wind made moan;
Earth stood hard as iron,
Water like a stone;
Snow had fallen, snow on snow,
Snow on snow,
In the bleak mid-winter
Long ago.

Our God, heaven cannot hold Him
Nor earth sustain,
Heaven and earth shall flee away
When He comes to reign:
In the bleak mid-winter
A stable-place sufficed
The Lord God Almighty —
Jesus Christ.

Enough for Him, whom Cherubim
Worship night and day,
A breastful of milk
And a manger full of hay;
Enough for Him, whom Angels
Fall down before,
The ox and ass and camel
Which adore.

Angels and Archangels
May have gathered there,
Cherubim and seraphim
Thronged the air;
But only His Mother
In her maiden bliss
Worshipped the Beloved
With a kiss.

What can I give Him,
Poor as I am?
If I were a Shepherd
I would bring a lamb;
If I were a Wise Man
I would do my part,
Yet what I can I give Him,
Give my heart.

Text: Christina Rossetti, ca. 1872.

Music: Gustav Holst, ca. 1906.

It Came Upon a Midnight Clear

(Verse)

It came upon the midnight clear,
That glorious song of old.
From angels bending near the earth,
To touch their harps of gold.

Peace on the earth, good will to men,
From heaven's all-gracious King.
The world in solemn stillness lay,
To hear the angels sing.

(Verse)

Still through the cloven skies they come,
With peaceful wings unfurled.
And still their heavenly music floats,
Over all the weary world.

Above its sad and lowly plains,
They bend on hovering wing.
And ever over its babel-sounds,
The blessed angels sing.

(Verse)
Yet with the woes of sin and strife,
The world has suffered long.
Beneath the heavenly strain have rolled,
Two thousand years of wrong.

And man at war with man hears not,
The tidings which they bring.
O hush the noise, ye men of strife,
And hear the angels sing.

(Verse)
O ye, beneath life's crushing load,
Whose forms are bending low.
Who toil along the climbing way,
With painful steps and slow.

Look now, for glad and golden hours,
Come swiftly on the wing.
O rest beside the weary road,
And hear the angels sing.

(Verse)
For lo, the days are hastening on,
By prophets seen of old.
When with the ever-circling years,
Shall come the time foretold.

When peace shall over all the earth,
Its ancient splendors fling.
And the whole world give back the song,
Which now the angels sing.

Text: Edmund H. Sears, ca. 1849
Music: Richard S. Willis, ca. 1850.

Jingle Bells

(Verse)

Dashing through the snow,
In a one-horse open sleigh.
O'er the fields we go,
Laughing all the way.
Bells on bob tails ring,
Making spirits bright.
What fun it is to laugh and sing,
A sleighing song tonight.

(Chorus)

Oh, jingle bells, jingle bells,
Jingle all the way.
Oh, what fun it is to ride,
In a one-horse open sleigh.
Jingle bells, jingle bells,
Jingle all the way.
Oh, what fun it is to ride,
In a one-horse open sleigh.

(Verse)

A day or two ago,
I thought I'd take a ride.
And soon Miss Fanny Bright,
Was seated by my side.
The horse was lean and lank,
Misfortune seemed his lot.
We got into a drifted bank,
And then we got upset.

(Chorus)

Oh, jingle bells, jingle bells,
Jingle all the way.
Oh, what fun it is to ride,
In a one-horse open sleigh.
Jingle bells, jingle bells,
Jingle all the way.
Oh, what fun it is to ride,
In a one-horse open sleigh.

Text: James Lord Pierpont, ca. 1850.

Music: James Lord Pierpont, ca. 1850.

Jolly Old St. Nicholas

(Verse)

Jolly old St. Nicholas,
Lean your ear this way!
Don't you tell a single soul,
What I'm going to say;
Christmas Eve is coming soon;
Now, you dear old man,
Whisper what you'll bring to me:
Tell me if you can.

(Verse)

When the clock is striking twelve,
When I'm fast asleep,
Down the chimney broad and black,
With your pack you'll creep;
All the stockings you will find
Hanging in a row;
Mine will be the shortest one,
You'll be sure to know.

(Verse)

Johnny wants a pair of skates, Susy wants a dolly;
Nellie wants a story book; She thinks dolls are
folly;
As for me, my little brain isn't very bright;
Choose for me, old Santa Claus. What you think
is right.

Text: Emily Huntington Miller, ca. 1865.
Music: James R. Murray, ca. 1874.

Joy To the World

(Verse)

Joy to the world, the Lord is come;
Let earth receive her King!
Let ev'ry heart prepare him room,

(Chorus)

And heaven and nature sing,
And heaven and nature sing,
And heaven, and heaven and nature sing.

(Verse)

Joy to the world, the Savior reigns!
Let men their songs employ;
While fields and floods, rocks, hills, and plains

(Chorus)

Repeat the sounding joy,
Repeat the sounding joy,
Repeat, repeat the sounding joy.

(Verse)

No more let sins and sorrow grow,
Nor thorns infest the ground;
He comes to make His blessings flow,

(Chorus)

Far as the curse was found,
Far as the curse was found,
Far as, far as the curse was found.

(Verse)

He rules the world with truth and grace,
And makes the nations prove.
The glories of His righteousness.

(Chorus)

And wonders of His love,
And wonders of His love,
And wonders, wonders, of His love.

Text: Isaac Watts, 1674–1748.
Music: George F. Handel, 1685–1759.

Lo, How a Rose E'er Blooming

(Verse)

Lo, how a Rose e'er blooming
From tender stem hath sprung!
Of Jesse's lineage coming
As men of old have sung.
It came, a flower bright,
Amid the cold of winter
When half-gone was the night.

(Verse)

Isaiah 'twas foretold it,
The Rose I have in mind:
With Mary we behold it,
The virgin mother kind.
To show God's love aright
She bore to men a Savior
When half-gone was the night.

(Verse)

This Flower, whose fragrance tender
With sweetness fills the air,
Dispels with glorious splendor
The darkness everywhere.
True man, yet very God,
From sin and death He saves us
And lightens every load.

Text: Michael Praetorius, ca. 1599.

Music: Michael Praetorius, ca. 1599.

Oh, Come All Ye Faithful

(Verse)

Oh, come, all ye faithful,
joyful and triumphant,
Oh, come ye, Oh, come ye to Bethlehem.
Come and behold him,
Born the king of angels.

(Chorus)

Oh, come let us adore him,
Oh, come let us adore him,
Oh, come let us adore him,
Christ the Lord.

(Verse)

Sing, choirs of angels,
Sing in exultation,
Sing, all ye citizens of heav'n above:
"Glory to God,

All glory in the highest!"
(Chorus)
Oh, come let us adore him,
Oh, come let us adore him,
Oh, come let us adore him,
Christ the Lord.

(Verse)
Yea, Lord, we greet thee,
Born this happy morning,
Jesus, to thee be all glory giv'n;
Son of the Father,
Now in flesh appearing.

(Chorus)
Oh, come let us adore him,
Oh, come let us adore him,
Oh, come let us adore him,
Christ the Lord.

Text: John F. Wade, ca. 1711-1786.

Music: John F. Wade, ca. 1711-1786.

O Christmas Tree

(Verse)

O Christmas Tree, O Christmas tree,
How lovely are your branches!
O Christmas Tree, O Christmas tree,
How lovely are your branches!
Not only green in summer's heat,
But also winter's snow and sleet.
O Christmas tree, O Christmas tree,
How lovely are your branches!

(Verse)

O Christmas Tree, O Christmas tree,
Of all the trees most lovely;
O Christmas Tree, O Christmas tree,
Of all the trees most lovely.
Each year you bring to us delight
With brightly shining Christmas light!
O Christmas Tree, O Christmas tree,
Of all the trees most lovely.

(Verse)

O Christmas Tree, O Christmas tree,
We learn from all your beauty;
O Christmas Tree, O Christmas tree,
We learn from all your beauty.
Your bright green leaves with festive cheer,
Give hope and strength throughout the year.
O Christmas Tree, O Christmas tree,
We learn from all your beauty.

Text: Ernst Anschutz, ca. 1824.
Music: Melchior Franck, ca. 16th Century.

O Come, O Come, Emanuel

(Verse)

O come, O come, Immanuel,
And ransom captive Israel.
That mourns in lonely exile here,
Until the Son of God appear.

(Chorus)

Rejoice! Rejoice! Immanuel,
Shall come to you, O Israel.

(Verse)

O come, O Wisdom from on high,
Who ordered all things mightily;
To us the path of knowledge show,
And teach us in its ways to go.

(Chorus)

Rejoice! Rejoice! Immanuel,
Shall come to you, O Israel.

(Verse)

O come, O come, great Lord of might,
Who to your tribes on Sinai's height.
In ancient times did give the law,
In cloud and majesty and awe.

(Chorus)

Rejoice! Rejoice! Immanuel
Shall come to you, O Israel.

(Verse)

O come, O Branch of Jesse's stem,
Unto your own and rescue them!
From depths of hell your people save,
And give them victory o'er the grave.

(Chorus)

Rejoice! Rejoice! Immanuel
shall come to you, O Israel.

(Verse)

O come, O Key of David, come,
And open wide our heavenly home.
Make safe for us the heavenward road,
And bar the way to death's abode.

(Chorus)

Rejoice! Rejoice! Immanuel,
shall come to you, O Israel.

(Verse)

O come, O Bright and Morning Star,
And bring us comfort from afar!
Dispel the shadows of the night,
And turn our darkness into light.

(Chorus)

Rejoice! Rejoice! Immanuel,
Shall come to you, O Israel.

(Verse)

O come, O King of nations, bind
In one the hearts of all mankind.
Bid all our sad divisions cease
And be yourself our King of Peace.

(Chorus)

Rejoice! Rejoice! Immanuel
shall come to you, O Israel.

Text: Translator, John Mason Neale, ca. 1861.

Music: Veni Emmanuel, ca. 15th Century.

O Holy Night

(Verse)

O holy night! The stars are brightly shining,
It is the night of the dear Savior's birth.
Long lay the world in sin and error pining.
'Till He appeared and the soul felt its worth.
A thrill of hope the weary world rejoices,
For yonder breaks a new and glorious morn!

(Chorus)

Fall on your knees!
O hear the angel voices!
O night divine,
O night when Christ was born,
O night, O holy night, O night divine!

(Verse)

Led by the light of faith serenely beaming,
With glowing hearts by His cradle we stand.
So led by light of a star sweetly gleaming,
Here come the wise men from Orient land.
The King of Kings lay thus in lowly manger,
In all our trials born to be our friend.

(Chorus)

He knows our need,
To our weakness no stranger,
Behold your King!
Before Him lowly bend!
Behold your King! Your King!
Before him lowly bend!

Verse)

Truly He taught us to love one another,
His law is love and His gospel is peace.
Chains shall he break,
For the slave is our brother.
And in his name all oppression shall cease.
Sweet hymns of joy in grateful chorus raise we,
With all our hearts we praise His holy name.

(Chorus)

Christ is the Lord!
Then ever! Ever praise we!
His power and glory evermore proclaim!
His power and glory evermore proclaim!

O Little Town of Bethlehem

(Verse)

O little town of Bethlehem,

How still we see thee lie.

Above thy deep and dreamless sleep,

The silent stars go by;

Yet in thy dark streets shineth,

The everlasting Light.

The hopes and fears of all the years,

Are met in thee tonight.

(Verse)

For Christ is born of Mary,

And, gathered all above.

While mortals sleep, the angels keep

Their watch of wond'ring love.

O morning stars, together

Proclaim the holy birth,

And praises sing to God the King,

And peace to men on earth.

(Verse)

How silently, how silently
The wondrous gift is giv'n!
So God imparts to human hearts
The blessings of his heav'n.
No ear may hear his coming;
But in this world of sin,
Where meek souls will receive him, still
The dear Christ enters in.

Text: Phillips Brooks, 1835–1893

Music: Lewis H. Redner, 1831–1908

Once in Royal David's City

(Verse)

Once in Royal David's city
Stood a lowly cattle shed,
Where a mother laid her Baby
In a manger for His bed:
Mary was that mother mild,
Jesus Christ her little Child.

(Verse)

He came down to earth from heaven,
Who is God and Lord of all,
And His shelter was a stable,
And His cradle was a stall;
With the poor, and mean, and lowly,
Lived on earth our Saviour holy.

(Verse)

And through all His wondrous childhood
He would honour and obey,
Love and watch the lowly maiden,
In whose gentle arms He lay:
Christian children all must be
Mild, obedient, good as He.

(Verse)

For he is our childhood's pattern;
Day by day, like us He grew;
He was little, weak and helpless,
Tears and smiles like us He knew;
And He feeleth for our sadness,
And He shareth in our gladness.

(Verse)

And our eyes at last shall see Him,
Through His own redeeming love;
For that Child so dear and gentle
Is our Lord in heaven above,
And He leads His children on
To the place where He is gone.

(Verse)

Not in that poor lowly stable,
With the oxen standing by,
We shall see Him; but in heaven,
Set at God's right hand on high;
Where like stars His children crowned
All in white shall wait around.

Text: Cecil Frances Alexander, ca. 1848.
Music: Henry John Gauntlett, ca. 1849.

Silent Night

(Verse)

Silent night! Holy night!
All is calm, all is bright,
Round yon virgin mother and Child.
Holy Infant, so tender and mild,
Sleep in heavenly peace;
Sleep in heavenly peace.

(Verse)

Silent night! Holy night!
Shepherds quake at the sight!
Glories stream from heaven afar;
Heav'nly hosts sing Alleluia!
Christ, the Savior, is born!
Christ, the Savior, is born!

(Verse)

Silent night! Holy night!
Son of God, love's pure light
Radiant beams from thy holy face,
With the dawn of redeeming grace,
Jesus, Lord, at thy birth;
Jesus, Lord, at thy birth.

Text: Joseph Mohr, 1792–1848)
Music: Franz Gruber, 1787–1863

 Toyland

(Verse)

Toyland, toyland,
Little girl and boy land.
While you dwell within it,
You are ever happy there.,

(Chorus)

Childhood's joy land
Mystic merry toyland.
Once you pass its borders,
You can ne'er return again.

(Verse)

When you've grown up, my dears,
And are as old as I.
You'll laugh and ponder on the years,
That roll so swiftly by, my dears,
That roll so swiftly by.

(Chorus)
Childhood's joy land,
Mystic merry toyland.
Once you pass its borders,
You can ne'er return again.

Text: Victor Herbert and Glen Macdonough, ca. 1903.

Music: Victor Herbert and Glen Macdonough, ca. 1903.

The Twelve Days of Christmas

(Verse)

On the first day of Christmas,
my true love sent to me:
A Partridge in a Pear Tree.

(Verse)

On the second day of Christmas,
my true love sent to me:
2 Turtle Doves,
and a Partridge in a Pear Tree.

(Verse)

On the third day of Christmas,
my true love sent to me:
3 French Hens,
2 Turtle Doves,
and a Partridge in a Pear Tree.

(Verse)

On the fourth day of Christmas,
my true love sent to me:
4 Calling Birds,
3 French Hens,
2 Turtle Doves,
and a Partridge in a Pear Tree.

(Verse)

On the fifth day of Christmas,
my true love sent to me:
5 Golden Rings,
4 Calling Birds,
3 French Hens,
2 Turtle Doves,
and a Partridge in a Pear Tree.

(Verse)

On the sixth day of Christmas
my true love sent to me:
6 Geese a Laying,
5 Golden Rings,

4 Calling Birds,
3 French Hens,
2 Turtle Doves,
and a Partridge in a Pear Tree.

(Verse)

On the seventh day of Christmas,
my true love sent to me:
7 Swans a Swimming,
6 Geese a Laying,
5 Golden Rings,
4 Calling Birds,
3 French Hens,
2 Turtle Doves,
and a Partridge in a Pear Tree.

(Verse)

On the eighth day of Christmas,
my true love sent to me:
8 Maids a Milking,
7 Swans a Swimming,
6 Geese a Laying,

5 Golden Rings,
4 Calling Birds,
3 French Hens,
2 Turtle Doves,
and a Partridge in a Pear Tree.

(Verse)
On the ninth day of Christmas,
my true love sent to me:
9 Ladies Dancing,
8 Maids a Milking,
7 Swans a Swimming,
6 Geese a Laying,
5 Golden Rings,
4 Calling Birds,
3 French Hens,
2 Turtle Doves,
and a Partridge in a Pear Tree.

(Verse)
On the tenth day of Christmas,
my true love sent to me:

10 Lords a Leaping,
9 Ladies Dancing,
8 Maids a Milking,
7 Swans a Swimming,
6 Geese a Laying,
5 Golden Rings,
4 Calling Birds,
3 French Hens,
2 Turtle Doves,
and a Partridge in a Pear Tree.

(Verse)
On the eleventh day of Christmas,
my true love sent to me:
11 Pipers Piping,
10 Lords a Leaping,
9 Ladies Dancing,
8 Maids a Milking,
7 Swans a Swimming,
6 Geese a Laying,
5 Golden Rings,
4 Calling Birds,

3 French Hens,
2 Turtle Doves,
and a Partridge in a Pear Tree.

(Verse)
On the twelfth day of Christmas,
my true love sent to me:
12 Drummers Drumming,
11 Pipers Piping,
10 Lords a Leaping,
9 Ladies Dancing,
8 Maids a Milking,
7 Swans a Swimming,
6 Geese a Laying,
5 Golden Rings,
4 Calling Birds,
3 French Hens,
2 Turtle Doves,
and a Partridge in a Pear Tree.

Text: Traditional with additions by Frederic Austin, ca. 1780.

Music: Traditional with additions by Frederic Austin, ca. 1780.

Up On the Housetop

(Verse)

Up on the housetop, reindeer pause
Out jumps good old Santa Claus;
Down through the chimney with lots of toys,
All for the little ones, Christmas joys.

(Chorus)

Ho, ho, ho! Who wouldn't go?
Ho, ho, ho! Who wouldn't go?
Up on the housetop, click, click, click,
Down through the chimney with good Saint
Nick.

(Verse)

First, comes the stocking of little Nell'
Oh, dear Santa, fill it well;
Give her a dolly that laughs and cries,
One that will open and shut her eyes.

(Chorus)

Ho, ho, ho! Who wouldn't go?
Ho, ho, ho! Who wouldn't go?
Up on the housetop, click, click, click,
Down through the chimney with good Saint
Nick.

(Verse)

Next, comes the stocking of little Will;
Oh, just see what a glorious fill!
Here is a hammer and lots of tacks,
Also a ball and a whip that cracks.

(Chorus)

Ho, ho, ho! Who wouldn't go?
Ho, ho, ho! Who wouldn't go?
Up on the housetop, click, click, click,
Down through the chimney with good Saint
Nick.

Text: Benjamin Hanby, ca. 1864.

Music: Benjamin Hanby, ca. 1864.

We Three Kings

(Verse)

We three kings of Orient are;
Bearing gifts we traverse afar,
Field and fountain, moor and mountain,
Following yonder star.

(Chorus)

O star of wonder, star of light,
Star with royal beauty bright,
Westward leading, still proceeding,
Guide us to thy perfect light.

(Verse)

Born a King on Bethlehem's plain,
Gold I bring to crown him again,
King forever, ceasing never,
Over us all to reign.

(Chorus)

O star of wonder, star of light,
Star with royal beauty bright,
Westward leading, still proceeding,
Guide us to thy perfect light.

(Verse)

Frankincense to offer have I;
Incense owns a Deity nigh;
Prayer and praising, voices raising,
Worshiping God on high.

(Chorus)

O star of wonder, star of light,
Star with royal beauty bright,
Westward leading, still proceeding,
Guide us to thy perfect light.

(Verse)

Myrrh is mine; its bitter perfume
Breathes a life of gathering gloom;
Sorrowing, sighing, bleeding, dying,
Sealed in the stone-cold tomb.

(Chorus)

O star of wonder, star of light,
Star with royal beauty bright,
Westward leading, still proceeding,
Guide us to thy perfect light.

(Verse)

Glorious now behold him arise;
King and God and sacrifice:
Alleluia, Alleluia,
Sounds through the earth and skies.

(Chorus)

O star of wonder, star of light,
Star with royal beauty bright,
Westward leading, still proceeding,
Guide us to thy perfect light.

Music: John Henry Hopkins Jr., ca. 1857.

Text: John Henry Hopkins Jr., ca. 1857.

We Wish You a Merry Christmas

(Verse)

We wish you a merry Christmas,
We wish you a merry Christmas,
We wish you a merry Christmas and a happy
New year.

(Chorus)

Good tidings we bring to you and your kin,
We wish you a merry Christmas and a happy
New year.

(Verse)

Oh, bring us some figgy pudding,
Oh, bring us some figgy pudding,
Oh, bring us some figgy pudding,
And bring it right here.

(Chorus)

Good tidings we bring to you and your kin,
We wish you a merry Christmas and a happy
New year.

(Verse)

We won't go until we get some,
We won't go until we get some,
We won't go until we get some,
So bring it right here.

(Chorus)

Good tidings we bring to you and your kin,
We wish you a merry Christmas and a happy
New year.

(Verse)

We all like our figgy pudding,
We all like our figgy pudding,
We all like our figgy pudding,
With all its good cheers.

(Chorus)

Good tidings we bring to you and your kin,
We wish you a merry Christmas and a happy
New year.

(Verse)

We wish you a merry Christmas,
We wish you a merry Christmas,
We wish you a merry Christmas and a happy
New year.

Text: Arthur Warrell, 1935.

Music: Arthur Warrell, 1935.

What Child Is This?

(Verse)

What Child is this, who laid to rest,
On Mary's lap is sleeping?
Whom angels greet with anthems sweet,
While shepherds watch are keeping?

(Chorus)

This, this is Christ, the King,
Whom shepherds guard and angels sing:
Haste, haste to bring Him laud,
The Babe, the Son of Mary!

(Verse)

Why lies He in such mean estate,
Where ox and ass are feeding?
Good Christian, fear: for sinners here
The silent Word is pleading.

(Chorus)

This, this is Christ, the King,
Whom shepherds guard and angels sing:
Haste, haste to bring Him laud,
The Babe, the Son of Mary!

(Verse)

So bring Him incense, gold, and myrrh,
Come, peasant, king to own Him.
The King of kings salvation brings;
Let loving hearts enthrone Him.

(Chorus)

This, this is Christ, the King,
Whom shepherds guard and angels sing:
Haste, haste to bring Him laud,
The Babe, the Son of Mary!

Text: William Chatterton Dix, ca. 1865.

Music: Traditional English tune of "Greensleeves."

While Shepherds Watched Their Flocks

(Verse)

While shepherds watch'd their flocks by night,
All seated on the ground,
The angel of the Lord came down,
And glory shone around.
"Fear not," said he, for mighty dread
Had seized their troubled mind;
"Glad tidings of great joy I bring
To you and all mankind."

(Verse)

"To you, in David's town this day,
Is born of David's line
The Savior who is Christ the Lord,
And this shall be the sign:
The heav'nly Babe you there shall find
To human view displayed,
All meanly wrapped in swathing bands,
And in a manger laid."

(Verse)

Thus spake the seraph, and forthwith
Appeared a shining throng
Of angels praising God, who thus
Addressed their joyful song:
"All glory be to God on high
And on the earth be peace.
Goodwill henceforth from heav'n to men
Begin and never cease."

Text: Nahum Tate, ca. 1700.
Music, Yorkshire Carol, ca. 1800.

Made in United States
Orlando, FL
14 December 2021